WITHDRAWN

THE SILK ROUTE

7,000 MILES OF HISTORY

by John S. Major

illustrated by Stephen Fieser

HarperCollins*Publishers*

BYZANTIUM

BLACK SEA

CASPIAN SEA

TRANS

Rome

Byzantium

Damascus

Baghdad

Hera

MEDITERRANEAN SEA

Tyre

Jerusalem

PERSI

SAHARA DESERT

ARABIA

NILE RIVER

AFRICA

Mecca

ARABIAN

| 0 | | 500 | | 1,000 miles |

| 0 | 500 | 1,000 | 1,500 kilometers |

The Silk Route *7,000 Miles of History* Text copyright © 1995 by John S. Major Illustrations copyright © 1995 by Stephen Fieser

Library of Congress Cataloging-in-Publication Data

Major, John S.   The silk route : 7,000 miles of history / by John S. Major ; illustrated by Stephen Fieser.   p.   cm.
  Summary: Traces the history and purpose of the legendary trade route between China and Byzantium during the Tang Dynasty (A.D. 618–906).
  ISBN 0-06-022924-1. — ISBN 0-06-022926-8 (lib. bdg.)
  1. Silk Road—History—Pictorial works—Juvenile literature.   [1. Silk Road—History.   2. Trade routes—Asia—History.]   I. Fieser, Stephen,
ill. II. Title.   DS33.1.M35   1995   950'.1—dc20   92-38169   CIP   AC

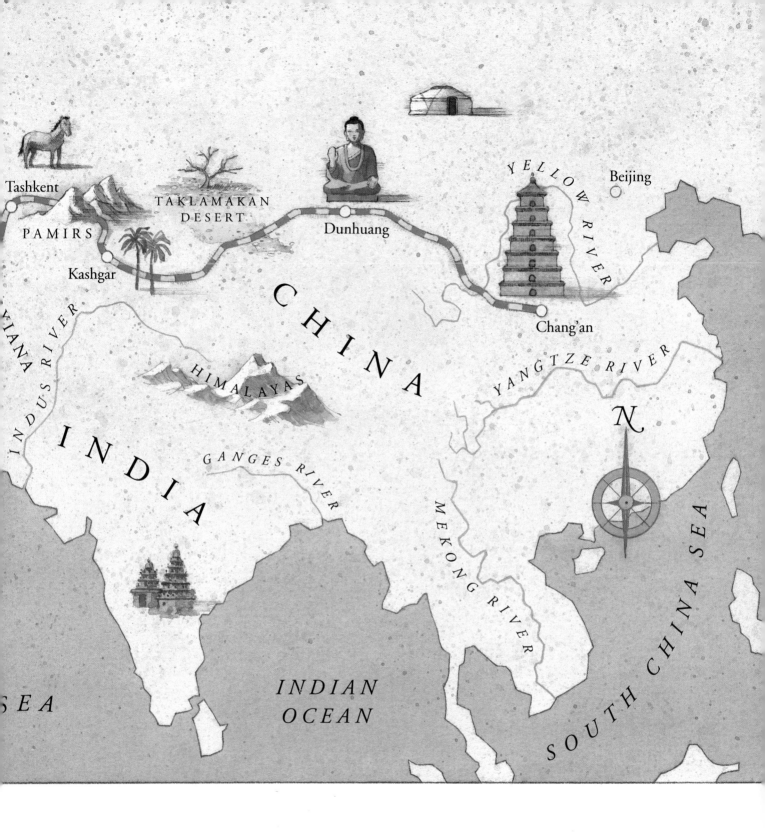

IN MEMORIAM:
Kathryn Demarest Major
Walter George Fieser

A.D. 700 . . .

The Roman Empire has fallen. Italy, Spain, and northern Europe are controlled by Germanic tribes. London and Paris are small towns; Rome is a half-deserted city of ruins.

In the eastern Mediterranean, the Roman tradition lives on in the Byzantine Empire, with its capital at the great city of Byzantium (also called Constantinople; now Istanbul).

The Christian rulers of Byzantium face a serious challenge from the rapidly expanding world of Islam. Founded by the Prophet Muhammad in 622, Islam has

spread throughout Arabia and now also controls Iraq, Armenia, Persia, and much of North Africa.

Meanwhile, on the other side of the world, China is ruled by the glorious Tang Dynasty (618–906), whose emperors have brought China to a high point of power, territorial control, and cultural brilliance. China's capital, Chang'an, is the largest city in the world.

The great empires of the West and the East are linked by the Silk Route, an ancient trade network of caravan tracks across the steppes and deserts of Central Asia.

Tang Dynasty China, A.D. 700

The Chinese people called their country the Middle Kingdom. But people in the West called China the Land of Silk. Among all of China's many gifts to world civilization— paper, printing, gunpowder, and a great deal more—silk was the most highly prized in the ancient Western world.

Silk cloth was invented in China around 3000 B.C. No one knows who first made silk cloth. Many Chinese people believed that it was invented by the Silkworm Empress. She was the wife of the Yellow Emperor, the mythical founder of Chinese civilization.

On farms all over China men grow grain while women produce silk. They tend groves of mulberry trees and feed the leaves to silkworms. When the silkworms mature, they make cocoons of silk, which the women collect and boil. Then the women unreel the delicate strand of silk from each cocoon, spin it into thread, and weave it into silk cloth. Farmers pay their taxes in grain and silk.

Chang'an

During the Tang Dynasty, bolts of plain white silk cloth of standard width and length were used as a kind of money. The government used silk to pay officials' salaries, and also exported silk along the Silk Route to Central Asia, where it was traded for fine horses for the imperial army.

In the capital city of Chang'an, merchants get a caravan ready to go to the West. Officials watch while workers take bolts of silk from a government

warehouse and load them onto camels. The merchants who will join the caravan buy many things in the city market to trade privately along the way. These trade goods include porcelain, dried rhubarb and other herbal medicines, and fancy silk cloth woven in colors and patterns especially designed to suit the tastes of the Islamic and Byzantine worlds.

The journey begins

The caravan includes many private merchants as well as Chinese government officials. Like the covered-wagon trains of the American West, members of the caravan travel together to help one another on the long, dangerous journey. Along the way they will face heat, hunger, thirst, and the ever-present possibility of bandit raids.

Few members of the original caravan will travel all the way to the Mediterranean. The silk and other goods that they are bringing from China will change hands several times along the way.

The caravan begins its journey, which will take many months. It is early spring. The caravan must get beyond the fierce western deserts before the heat of summer arrives. Leaving the city walls of Chang'an behind, it passes through rich farmland. A Buddhist temple is on a nearby hillside.

CHINESE: SI
silk, silk thread

Dunhuang

The Buddhist religion came to China from India along the Silk Route around A.D. 100. The oasis town of Dunhuang, for centuries an important trading and supply center for caravans, soon grew into a great religious center as well. Hundreds of Buddhist cave-temples were cut into the soft rock of a nearby cliff. The cave-temples contain Buddhist statues; the walls are decorated with bright religious paintings.

Some of the merchants go to the cave-temples of Dunhuang to pray for a safe journey, while others buy supplies in the town market. Some Chinese officials take charge of a small herd of horses brought from the west by another caravan. They will escort the horses back to the capital; other officials will continue west to purchase still more of them.

Taklamakan

The Taklamakan is one of the world's driest deserts. Its name means "if you go in, you won't come out" in Uighur Turkish, one of the main languages of Central Asia. The caravan skirts the northern edge of the desert, just south of the snow-capped peaks of the Tian Shan Mountains. The route is very rough, passing around sand dunes, across rocky flats, and through tangled willow thickets along dry riverbeds. But the caravan's two-humped Bactrian camels are

strong and hardy. They are used to this difficult country.

Many of the camels and camel drivers that set out from Chang'an turned back at Dunhuang. The merchants hired new ones for this stage of the journey, along with extra animals to carry food and water for crossing the desert. Such changes of men and animals will occur several times along the way from China to Damascus.

Kashgar

Hot and tired after their trip across the Taklamakan Desert, the men and animals hurry to reach the oasis city of Kashgar. The pastures near the city are dotted with grazing animals and the camps of herding peoples: Uighurs in round felt yurts, Turkomans and Tibetans in black tents.

Kashgar is famous for its fruit. Dates, melons, and grapes are grown in irrigated fields and vineyards. Everyone in the caravan looks forward to fresh food and water.

Some of the Chinese members of the caravan will end their journey here. They trade silk for dried dates, raisins, jade, and other local products to bring back to China. Others will continue on toward the west, joined by new merchants, guards, and camel drivers with fresh animals from Kashgar.

The Pamirs

The Pamirs are a range of high mountains in eastern Afghanistan. Here the route winds through narrow, high-walled valleys beside rushing rivers. The camel drivers call this section of the Silk Route the "Trail of Bones" because of the many men and animals that have died along the way from falls and from sudden storms in the high, cold passes. The westbound caravan meets a caravan heading for China with luxury goods from Western lands and a herd of fine horses from Ferghana.

PERSIAN: *ABRASHAM*
silk

Tashkent, Kingdom of Ferghana

In the central market of Tashkent, the last remaining Chinese officials in the caravan trade bolts of silk for horses that they will take back to China. The horses of Ferghana are considered by Chinese military leaders to be the strongest and toughest in the world.

Tashkent marks the eastern edge of the Persian cultural world. Some private merchants trade Chinese silk, porcelain, and other goods for Persian metalwork, glass, and musical instruments. They too will head back to China from here.

Transoxiana

After making another stop, in the city of Samarkand, the caravan enters the wild country east of the Oxus (Amu Darya) River. No government rules this land; the nomads who live here will rob caravans if they get a chance to.

Suddenly the caravan is attacked by a group of Turkoman bandits on

horseback. After a fierce fight with swords and bows and arrows, the bandits are driven off. But some members of the caravan have been killed or wounded, and the bandits escape with a few heavily laden camels.

Herat

In this thriving Persian city, artisans produce fine metalwork, glassware, carpets, and other goods that can be sold for a high price in China. Herat is also, for the moment, on the eastern edge of the rapidly expanding Islamic world. A newly built mosque looms over the city market.

Merchants from the caravan mingle in the market with local merchants and Turkoman nomads, as well as with Arabs from Baghdad and Damascus. Traders from India are here too, selling spices and brightly dyed Indian cloth. Muslim imams, Zoroastrian priests, Nestorian Christian priests, and Buddhist monks tend to the religious needs of the cosmopolitan city.

The caravan will leave its last Bactrian camels in Herat. For the rest of the journey they will use dromedaries, the one-humped camels of Western Asia.

Baghdad

Baghdad is the greatest city of the Islamic world and a hub of world trade. Caravans crowd the roads leading to the city. An Arab merchant leads a group of African slaves bringing ivory, gold, and spices from Zanzibar. Ships coming upriver from the port at Basra bring spices and printed cotton cloth from India, pearls from the Persian Gulf, and precious stones from Ceylon (now Sri Lanka). Some of these goods will soon be heading east to China.

Only a handful of Chinese merchants remained with the caravan, and they will end their journey here. Most of the silk, porcelain, and other products from China have already changed hands several times along the way, increasing in value each time. The last remaining Chinese merchants will sell their goods for a fortune in Baghdad, but then they face a long, difficult, and dangerous trip home again.

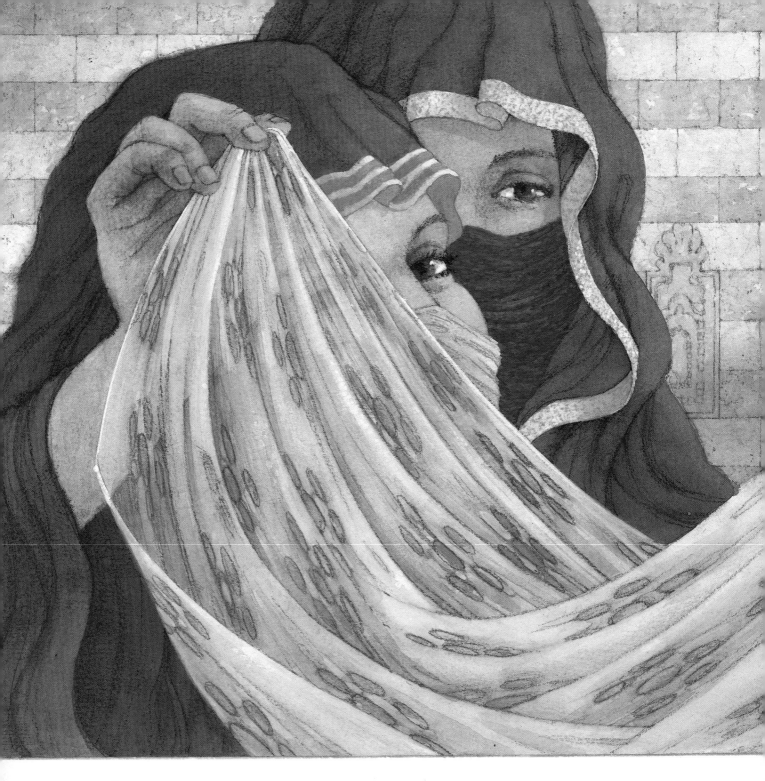

Damascus

Arab merchants have brought bolts of silk from Baghdad to Damascus. Only the finest silk cloth has traveled this far; it includes intricately patterned brocades, brilliantly colored satins, and thin gauze to make nightgowns for aristocratic ladies. Wealthy Muslim women, heavily veiled, admire bolts of finished silk cloth in a shop.

Tyre

In the port city of Tyre, on the Mediterranean coast of Lebanon, goods are loaded on ships bound for cities farther to the west. Some of the silk that was traded in the market at Damascus will be sent to Byzantium, the capital of the Eastern Roman Empire.

ΣΕΡΙΚΟΝ

GREEK: SERIKON
silk cloth

Byzantium

In the main hall of a splendid palace, a Byzantine nobleman receives a visit from a bishop of the Orthodox Christian church. Both are dressed in rich garments of silk brocade. The palace women remain in an inner courtyard, out of sight of the men. A visiting prince from Russia, far to the north, awaits his turn to speak to the nobleman. Perhaps he will receive a small present of silk to take back home with him.

The garments worn by the wealthy people of Byzantium are made of silk

cloth brought from China, more than 6,000 miles away. Few people in Byzantium have more than a vague idea of where China is or what its people are like, just as few Chinese know anything about the Eastern Roman Empire. Yet Chinese silk is sold in Byzantium, and Byzantine gold coins circulate in the markets of China. The two empires are linked together by trade, thanks to the brave and enterprising merchants of the Silk Route.

A Closer Look

Silk • For thousands of years the painstaking process of raising silkworms and making cloth from their cocoons had been a Chinese monopoly. But around A.D. 550, during the reign of the Eastern Roman Emperor Justinian, two Nestorian Christian monks who had traveled to China returned to Syria, smuggling back with them silkworm eggs hidden in their hollow bamboo walking sticks. This allowed a silk industry to be established in the Middle East, undercutting the market for ordinary-grade Chinese silk. However, high-quality silk textiles, woven in China especially for the Middle Eastern market, continued to bring high prices in Damascus and Byzantium, and trade along the Silk Route therefore continued as before.

Chang'an • Located in the valley of the Wei River, a tributary of the Yellow River, the Tang capital of Chang'an had been the most important city in China for over 1000 years. Located at the eastern end of the Silk Route as well as near the Great Wall that marked the boundary between China and the nomadic tribes of the north, the city guarded China's most important strategic interests. Chang'an, with a population of well over a million people, was famous throughout East Asia for its palaces, parks, temples, schools, and restaurants. The city was a hub of world trade, and it included resident populations of merchants, scholars, and religious leaders from as far away as Korea, Japan, India, Persia, Armenia, and Syria.

China's Door to the West • The rich agricultural lands of China are isolated from the rest of mainland Asia by high mountains, steep valleys, deserts, and grasslands. The corridor formed by the Wei River and the upper reaches of the Yellow River marked a natural highway that pierced the veil of China's natural isolation. During the Tang Dynasty this corridor was carefully kept under Chinese control and guarded against raids by Tibetans to the south and Turkic tribes to the north. A western extension of the Great Wall was marked by guard towers furnished with beacon fires that could bring news of danger to Chang'an in a matter of hours.

Buddhism • Buddhism was founded in northern India by Gautama, the Buddha ("Enlightened One"), around 550 B.C. Buddhists believed that a life of prayer, meditation, and good works could free the soul from attachment to the sinful world. Buddhism soon spread throughout India and into Central Asia, entering China along the Silk Route around A.D. 100. Over the next few centuries it became established in China and was accepted as one of that country's three major religions (along with Confucianism and Taoism). The early Tang Dynasty marked a time of particular power and influence of Buddhism in China. Cave-temples such as those at Dunhuang (also spelled Tun-huang) attracted pilgrims from all over East Asia.

Caravan Life • Caravans were made up of many groups of both private merchants and government officials. The travelers hired professional camel drivers, baggage handlers, camp tenders, and other workers, all of whom typically worked only one relatively short stretch of the entire route. Private merchants hired their own armed guards; the Chinese government officials who traveled between Chang'an and Tashkent had military escorts. The caravans carried supplies of food, water, and animal fodder for crossing the deserts that lay in their path. Depending on the terrain, they might go as few as ten or as many as fifty miles in a day. Each night the travelers pitched tents, hobbled their camels, and set out guards to secure their camp against bandit raids.

Oasis Cities • Within the dry and barren lands between China and the Middle East are a few large oases, isolated pockets of abundant water that make agriculture and urban life possible. Walled cities were surrounded by irrigated fields and pasturelands. Such cities as Kashgar, Bactra (now Balkh), and Samarkand became the capitals of substantial kingdoms as well as great centers of trade along the Silk Route. The Silk Route itself was a network of trails rather than a single highway; branches of the route led from oasis to oasis and to market centers in India, Persia, Russia, and the Middle East.

The oasis cities were surrounded by populations of nomadic herding peoples who traded animal products, such as wool, meat, and hides, for urban goods such as grain and metalware. These nomadic tribes were only loosely under the control of the oasis kingdoms and were feared by townspeople and caravan merchants.

Invasion Routes of Inner Asia • In some sections of Central Asia geography forced the Silk Route trade to flow through narrow and well-defined corridors. Travelers from China to the Middle East could not avoid the dangerous rivers and high mountain passes of the Pamirs; trade between Afghanistan and India had to cross the Khyber Pass. Many times in history these strategic routes carried invading armies as well as peaceful caravans. Alexander the Great's armies reached the Pamirs in the third century B.C.; the Mongol hordes of Genghis Khan rode through them 1500 years later. As late as the nineteenth century Great Britain and Russia competed to control the invasion routes of inner Asia, the meeting point of the great civilizations of China, India, and the Middle East.

Nomad Warfare • The various nomadic tribes of Central Asia shared a common culture based on tending herds of grazing animals. The men of the tribes were trained from infancy to become expert fighters and hunters from horseback. Their primary duty was to guard the tribe's herds, but they would also raid towns and caravans whenever the opportunity presented itself. Their main weapon was the short, recurved, composite bow, made of wood and horn, with which they could fire volleys of armor-piercing arrows at full gallop: they used lances and swords for close combat. They specialized in lightning-fast attacks, taking their targets by surprise.

The cavalry units of China's imperial army adopted these nomad techniques of warfare to defend the empire's northern frontier. This led to China's almost insatiable demand for the strong, fast, hardy horses of Ferghana, one of the main items of trade along the Silk Route.

The Religions of Central Asia • Central Asian trading cities such as Herat were multicultural centers that reflected in population, culture, and religious beliefs the diversity of the peoples of Asia. Buddhists from eastern Afghanistan, Turkestan, and as far away as Nepal and China mingled with Hindus from India. Zoroastrianism, the ancient religion of Persia—

whose adherents worshipped the forces of light that struggled against Satanic darkness, and maintained temples with sacred fires—was rapidly giving way to the militant, expanding new religion of Islam. Nestorianism, a Syrian form of Christianity, established churches and cathedrals in all the major cities of Central Asia. Pockets of Greek paganism remained among the colonies left behind by Alexander the Great's conquests almost a thousand years earlier. In the surrounding steppelands, nomads worshipped the Great Blue Sky and communicated with gods and spirits through shamans and healers.

Baghdad and World Trade • Baghdad, together with the port city of Basra at the mouth of the Tigris River, was a focal point of both maritime and caravan trade. Although some caravans from the Silk Route took a northern route from Merv through Armenia to reach Byzantium overland, many others headed south through Herat to Baghdad and Damascus. Arab sailors from the Persian Gulf dominated shipping in the Indian Ocean, trading in cloth from India, gemstones from Ceylon (Sri Lanka), spices from Indonesia, and gold, ivory, and slaves from the eastern coast of Africa. Baghdad grew rich

from trade; it soon became a great political center as well. In 751 the Umayyad Caliphate established its capital at Baghdad and claimed the right to rule the entire Islamic world.

The Islamic Expansion • Islam, founded by Muhammad in the Arabian cities of Mecca and Medina in 622, makes no distinction between religion and civic life. It considers the world to be divided into the *Dar ol'Islam*, the "world submissive to God," and the *Dar ol'Harb*, the "world at war with God." Those who acknowledge the authority of Allah, the one true God according to the teachings of Muhammad, submit to His rule in every aspect of life.

Islamic armies conquered by force but converted by persuasion; believers in other religions were tolerated, but only Muslims had full civil rights in the Islamic world. The Islamic world grew at a phenomenal pace, and by 700 extended from Tunisia to Afghanistan. For about a century before the establishment of the Umayyad Caliphate at Baghdad, Damascus was the center of the Islamic world. To its ancient status as a hub of north–south and east–west caravan routes was added a new status as a city of mosques and universities, a magnet for merchants and scholars.

Byzantium • With the gradual decline of Rome, power in the Roman Empire shifted eastward. An eastern capital was established at Byzantium by the Emperor Constantine in 330. The Germanic invasions of the western portion of the Roman Empire in the sixth century left Byzantium in control of what was left of the empire. The Orthodox Christian Byzantine emperors ruled Greece, western Turkey, the Balkan states, and parts of southern Italy and North Africa, but found their power constantly challenged by Germans in the west, Persians in the east, and, after 622, Arab Muslims in the east and south. Nevertheless, Byzantium itself resisted conquest until it was overrun by the Turks in 1453.

The Eastern Roman Empire was rich and cosmopolitan, and many of the goods that traveled across Asia along the Silk Route were destined for its markets. It was also a transfer center for trade to Europe proper, along maritime routes that extended throughout the Mediterranean and via overland routes along the Danube River to central Europe and up the Volga to Russia and the Baltic Sea. A Frankish nobleman in Paris or a Catholic bishop in Spain might well have worn garments of silk that traveled, via Byzantium, the 7,000 miles from China.